Written by
Kimberly Jordano and Tebra Corcoran

Editor: Kim Cernek
Illustrator: Darcy Tom
Cover Illustrator: Kim Graves
Cover Photographer: Michael Jarrett
Designers: Moonhee Pak and Terri Lamadrid
Cover Designer: Moonhee Pak
Art Director: Tom Cochrane
Project Director: Carolea Williams

Introduction

Sight Word Books: Level 1 features 30 cross-curricular mini-books with fun, predictable text that you reproduce and your students personalize to make their very own set of beginning readers. Because emergent readers need frequent, intensive opportunities to practice reading strategies, including the mastery of high-frequency words called sight words, the stories in this resource give students repeated practice reading and writing over 50 words (see list on page 8) that most commonly appear in print.

Sight Word Books: Level 1 provides you with ways to enhance your existing literacy program by giving students at all levels the opportunity to read and write sight words; learn about directionality (left-to-right orientation) and tracking (one-to-one correspondence); use picture clues and word patterns to read new words; develop comprehension skills; improve fluency; expand vocabulary; and spell new words. The mini-books are also excellent tools for exploring modeled reading, shared reading, independent reading, and guided reading.

Sight Word Books: Level 1 is the perfect complement to your regular reading program or English-as-a-second-language program. As an added bonus, you can strengthen your home–school connection by encouraging students to take home their mini-books to share with their family. This collection of sight word mini-books is sure to inspire in every student an enthusiasm for reading!

Getting Started

Choose a mini-book to use for a class lesson. Use the mini-books in sequence, or select those that fit into your current thematic unit of study. Then, adjust the challenge level of the text, if necessary (see below), and copy a set of pages for each student.

ASSEMBLING THE MINI-BOOKS AND READING STICKS

Fold each page of a mini-book backwards onto itself so that the blank side of the paper does not show. Staple the pages together in a construction paper cover so that the creased sides face out. This approach is recommended because the thick, folded pages are much easier for little fingers to turn!

Cut from construction paper or a greeting card envelope (cut widthwise) a 4" (10 cm) square for each student's mini-book. Glue to the inside front cover of each mini-book the side edges and bottom of the construction paper square or the back of the envelope to create a pocket. This pocket can hold a reading stick for students to use as they read the words in their mini-book. To make a reading stick, glue to the end of a craft stick a small object that relates to the theme of the mini-book. For example, use a sticker, an illustration cut from a bulletin board border, a student's class picture, a small plastic toy or other object (e.g., a dried bean for the *Watch My Garden Grow* mini-book), or a pattern reproduced, reduced, and cut from the pattern pages (139–144). The reading sticks reinforce one-to-one correspondence and are a fun, motivational tool.

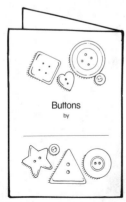

CUSTOMIZING THE CHALLENGE LEVEL

Sight Word Books: Level 1 includes two formats to help students practice reading and writing sight words. One sight word has been omitted from most of the sentences in the first four mini-books of each unit. This format encourages beginning readers and writers to follow the pattern of the text to identify the missing sight word and then write that word on the blank line. Only one sight word has been omitted from these books to give students repeated practice reading and writing a word that they will commonly see in print or use in their own writing. Have students use the sight word listed in the table of contents, or encourage students to write a word that they think best completes the sentences. More than one sight word has been omitted from most of the sentences in the fifth mini-book of each unit to give students an opportunity to review some of the sight words introduced in previous mini-books.

If students need a greater challenge with the mini-books, consider using liquid correction fluid or white labels to cover additional sight words in the text, draw blank lines in those places, and then make copies of the revised pages for the class.

Introducing a Mini-Book

Students can complete their mini-books in small groups or independently at a learning center. Another option is for the whole class to spend a week or so on each mini-book. Here is a sample plan.

Day One

Read aloud the book from the list of literature links on pages 9–18 that correlates with the mini-book you have chosen. Or, choose another book that matches the theme of the mini-book. Discuss the story and theme with the class.

Day Two

Copy on sentence strips the words from a mini-book. Cut apart the words, and place them in a pocket chart. Enlarge the pages of the mini-book, color and cut out the pictures, and place them above the words in the pocket chart. Read the mini-book to the class, and invite them to join you for a second reading. To extend learning, make another set of words and pictures, and give them to individual students to match to the words and pictures already in the pocket chart.

make ✫

Day Three

Review the pocket chart activities from the previous day. Then, give each student an assembled mini-book (see page 4). Invite students to write their name on the first page and the name of a person to whom they would like to dedicate their book on the second page. This simple activity gives students ownership of their book and inspires them to do thoughtful work. Tell students to write the missing sight word (word listed in the table of contents or another word they think best completes the sentence) on the blank lines and color the pictures on each page. Note that some pages feature blank paper dolls or other empty spaces for students to personalize. For example, students can glue a small class picture of themselves to the face of a paper doll and use crayons to color clothing on the body.

Day Four

Write the title of the mini-book on each student's construction paper cover. Then, invite students to write their name on and decorate the cover of their mini-book. Or, have students cut out the title from an extra copy of the first page, glue the title to their construction paper cover, write their name on the cover, and use art supplies and/or copies of the appropriate pattern on pages 139–144 to transform the cover into an art project. For example, students can glue die-cut leaves to the cover of *This Is Fall*, or they can color, cut out, and glue an egg copied from the Seasonal/Holiday Patterns on page 142 to the cover of *Spring Eggs*.

Day Five

Give each student a reading stick (see page 4) that coordinates with the mini-book. Invite students to use their stick to point to the words in the mini-book as they read. Then, have students take home their mini-book to share with their family and store in their book box (see page 6).

Parent Involvement

At the beginning of the year, send home with each student a copy of the Home–School Connection Letter (page 7). This letter describes how families can use the mini-books to become more directly involved in their child's reading development. The letter also describes a book box and a sight word box that can be used to organize all of the mini-books and sight word cards.

BOOK BOX

Encourage students to practice reading their books at home with family members. A great way to keep the books organized is to store them in a personalized book box. The Home–School Connection Letter asks parents to obtain a large plastic tub with a removable lid (a shoe box is too small). Invite students to use markers, paint, and stickers to decorate their box at home. For a special touch, insert each student's name into the frame _____'s Book Box, write it on a large label, and give students their label to take home along with their copy of the parent letter.

SIGHT WORD BOX

The Home–School Connection Letter asks parents to find a recipe box or other box that is large enough to hold more than 50 index cards. For each mini-book, have students write with their parents the new sight word or words on separate index cards and add the cards to their box. Remind students to practice reading their word cards to their family members.

Home-School Connection Letter

_____
Date

Dear Family,

We are beginning a program that will help your child learn to read and write over 50 words that appear most frequently in books. Examples of these words are *I, a, me, as,* and *have.* Learning to read these words by sight is an important strategy your child can use to become a strong, independent reader.

Each week or two, your child will bring home a mini-book that he or she has completed in class. Please ask your child to read this book to you each night. Beginning readers need frequent opportunities to practice reading.

Your child will complete 30 mini-books this year. Please find a plastic tub with a removable lid (a shoe box is too small), and help your child decorate it. Encourage your child to use this book box to store his or her mini-books. Also, please find a recipe box or other box that is large enough to hold more than 50 index cards. Each week, write on separate index cards the sight words featured in the latest mini-book, and place the cards in the sight word box. Encourage your child to practice reading these words at home.

Together, we can teach your child beginning reading skills and inspire him or her to love books!

Sincerely,

Sight Words List

a	for	make	this
all	from	may	to
am	go	me	up
an	good	my	was
and	has	not	we
are	have	on	went
as	here	one	what
at	I	say	where
be	in	see	who
but	is	that	will
can	it	the	with
could	like	there	yes
do	look	these	you

Mini-Book Overviews

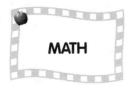

MATH

I Am

Literature Link: *Quick as a Cricket*
by Audrey and Don Wood
(CHILD'S PLAY)

Focus Word: am

Other Sight Words: a, an, as, I, me

Cover Art: Have students dip their hands in paint and stamp them on their cover.

Reading Stick: Use a small plastic ruler as a reading stick, or glue a paper ruler (page 139) to a craft stick.

Buttons

Literature Link: *Buttons, Buttons*
by Rozanne Lanczak Williams
(CREATIVE TEACHING PRESS)

Focus Word: we

Other Sight Words: and, have

Cover Art: Have students place buttons under their cover and rub a crayon over their cover to create a textured effect.

Reading Stick: Glue real or paper buttons (page 139) to a craft stick.

Look and See Shapes

Literature Link: *Bear in a Square*
by Stella Blackstone
(BAREFOOT BOOKS)

Focus Word: can

Other Sight Words: a, and, be, look, see, we, what, you

Cover Art: Have students glue to their cover shapes cut from construction paper.

Reading Stick: Glue a small plastic or real magnifying glass or a circle sticker to a craft stick.

Patterns

Literature Link: *Patterns All around Me*
by Trisha Callella-Jones
(CREATIVE TEACHING PRESS)

Focus Word: are

Other Sight Words: a, I, make, on, the, there

Cover Art: Have students use rubber or sponge stamps to make a pattern on their cover.

Reading Stick: Glue a scrap of patterned wallpaper or fabric or a real or paper birthday candle (page 139) to a craft stick.

Chef ____'s Pizza

Literature Link: *"Hi, Pizza Man!"*
by Virginia Walter
(ORCHARD BOOKS)

Focus Words: and, are, I, we

Other Sight Words: can, have, like, my, on, the, these

Cover Art: Have students color with a red crayon a paper pizza (page 139), glue shredded white paper cheese on the pizza, and then glue the pizza to their cover.

Reading Stick: Glue a brown pom-pom meatball to a craft stick.

SELF-ESTEEM

Look!

Literature Link: *Whoever You Are*
by Mem Fox
(HARCOURT)

Focus Word: look

Other Sight Words: at, me

Cover Art: Have students glue wiggly eyes and yarn hair to a paper circle, draw a mouth and a nose on the circle, and then glue the "face" to their cover.

Reading Stick: Glue paper glasses (page 140) to a craft stick.

When I Grow Up

Literature Link: *I Like Me!* by Nancy Carlson
(HARCOURT)

Focus Word: be

Other Sight Words: a, an, but, I, may, me, will

Cover Art: Have students decorate a paper doll with accessories (page 140) and glue the doll to their cover.

Reading Stick: Glue a small photo of a student to a craft stick.

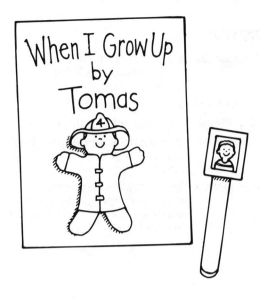

I Can

Literature Link: *I Am Special* by Kimberly Jordano
(CREATIVE TEACHING PRESS)

Focus Word: make

Other Sight Words: a, can, I, me

Cover Art: Have students use watercolors to paint a rainbow on their cover.

Reading Stick: Use a real paintbrush as a reading stick.

What Do We Need?

Literature Link: *What Do We Need?*
by Trisha Callella
(CREATIVE TEACHING PRESS)

Focus Word: do

Other Sight Words: we, yes

Cover Art: Have students glue to their cover paper triangles, squares, and rectangles in the shape of a house.

Reading Stick: Glue a heart sticker or a paper heart (page 140) to a craft stick.

Look at Me!

Literature Link: *I Can Read*
by Rozanne Lanczak Williams
(CREATIVE TEACHING PRESS)

Focus Words: look, make, me

Other Sight Words: a, at, can, do, I, my, this, what

Cover Art: Have students glue to their cover their photo glued on a paper square.

Reading Stick: Glue a small photo of each student or a paper book (page 140) to a craft stick.

SCIENCE

Watch My Garden Grow

Literature Link: *The Tiny Seed* by Eric Carle
(SIMON & SCHUSTER)

Focus Word: I

Other Sight Words: my, see, the

Cover Art: Have students glue to their cover a strip of green paper grass, green pipe cleaner stems, and flattened cupcake liners to make "flowers."

Reading Stick: Glue a real or paper seed (page 141) or a bean to a craft stick.

Rain

Literature Link: *Rain* by Robert Kalan
(MULBERRY BOOKS)

Focus Word: the

Other Sight Words: but, me, not, on

Cover Art: Have students paint dots of white paint on a blue cover and then drizzle small drops of water to streak the paint to make "rain."

Reading Stick: Glue a cocktail or paper umbrella (page 141) to a craft stick.

Bugs

Literature Link: *How Many Bugs Are in a Box?*
by David A. Carter
(SIMON & SCHUSTER)

Focus Word: is

Other Sight Words: it, that, there, where

Cover Art: Have students press their thumb in
ink, stamp it on their cover, and
then draws legs on the thumbprint
to make a "bug."

Reading Stick: Glue a plastic bug, a bug sticker,
or a paper bug (page 141) to a
craft stick.

Matter

Literature Link: *Apple Tree! Apple Tree!*
by Mary Blocksma
(CHILDREN'S PRESS)

Focus Word: a

Other Sight Words: is, me, this

Cover Art: Have students cut out from maga-
zines pictures of solids and liquids
and glue the pictures to their cover
to create a collage.

Reading Stick: Glue a small plastic or paper flower
(page 141) to a craft stick.

This Is Fall

Literature Link: *We Love Fall!*
by Diane Muldrow
(SCHOLASTIC)

Focus Words: I, is, on

Other Sight Words: me, see, that, the, this, will

Cover Art: Have students glue a paper tree
trunk and small paper leaves to
their cover.

Reading Stick: Glue a real or paper leaf (page 141)
to a craft stick.

Halloween Party

Literature Link: *Big Pumpkin*
by Erica Silverman
(ALADDIN)

Focus Word: was

Other Sight Words: a, do, like, one, you

Cover Art: Have students dip their foot in white paint, stamp it upside down on a dark-colored cover, and draw eyes and a mouth to make a "ghost."

Reading Stick: Wrap white tissue around a craft stick, and tie the tissue with string to make a "ghost." Or, glue a paper pumpkin (page 142) to a craft stick.

In Went

Literature Link: *Mousekin's Thanksgiving*
by Edna Miller
(PRENTICE HALL)

Focus Word: in

Other Sight Words: am, I, the, went

Cover Art: Have students glue corn kernels on a small paper plate and glue the plate to their cover.

Reading Stick: Use a real plastic fork as a reading stick, or glue a paper fork (page 142) to a craft stick.

A Valentine

Literature Link: *Love Bugs* by David A. Carter
(LITTLE SIMON)

Focus Word: it

Other Sight Words: a, be, could, for, is, one, this, you

Cover Art: Have students glue a foil heart and a paper doily to a red or pink cover.

Reading Stick: Glue a candy or paper heart (page 142) to a craft stick.

The Leprechaun

Literature Link: *St. Patrick's Day in the Morning* by Eve Bunting (CLARION)

Focus Word: here

Other Sight Words: a, for, is, me, to

Cover Art: Have students color with a green crayon a paper shamrock (page 142) and then glue the shamrock, foil coins, and gold glitter to their cover.

Reading Stick: Glue a shamrock sticker or a paper shamrock (page 142) to a craft stick.

Spring Eggs

Literature Link: *The Easter Egg Farm* by Mary Jane Auch (HOLIDAY HOUSE)

Focus Words: here, is, it

Other Sight Words: for, one, you

Cover Art: Have students glue to their cover shredded green paper and paper eggs (page 142) to make a "nest."

Reading Stick: Glue a jelly bean or an animal sticker to a craft stick.

ANIMALS

A Jungle Good Morning

Literature Link: *Rumble in the Jungle* by Giles Andreae (TIGER TALES)

Focus Word: to

Other Sight Words: good, I, in, say, the

Cover Art: Have students glue die-cut animals and green paper bushes to their cover.

Reading Stick: Glue an animal sticker, a small animal eraser, or a paper safari hat (page 143) to a craft stick.

At the Zoo

Literature Link: *We're Going to the Zoo*
by Tom Paxton
(MORROW)

Focus Word: will

Other Sight Words: are, at, I, see, the, where, you

Cover Art: Have students color a paper map (page 143) and glue it to their cover.

Reading Stick: Glue a jungle animal sticker or a paper safari hat (page 143) to a craft stick.

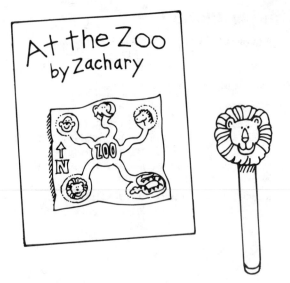

_____'s Farm

Literature Link: *One Cow Moo Moo!*
by David Bennett
(HENRY HOLT AND COMPANY)

Focus Word: like

Other Sight Words: all, I, that, the

Cover Art: Have students color a paper barn (page 143) and glue it to their cover.

Reading Stick: Glue wiggly eyes and a beak (cut from orange felt/paper) to a yellow pom-pom to make a "chick," and glue the chick to a craft stick.

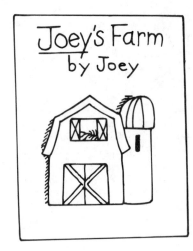

An Alligator

Literature Link: *Alligator Baby*
by Robert Munsch
(CARTWHEEL BOOKS®)

Focus Word: has

Other Sight Words: a, an, can, in, the

Cover Art: Have students color a paper alligator (page 143) and glue it to their cover.

Reading Stick: Glue a white triangle tooth to a craft stick.

All Penguins

Literature Link: *Tacky the Penguin* by Helen Lester (HOUGHTON MIFFLIN)

Focus Words: all, like, to, will

Other Sight Words: a, but, see, you

Cover Art: Have students color a paper penguin (page 143) and glue it to their cover.

Reading Stick: Glue a real or paper black feather to a craft stick.

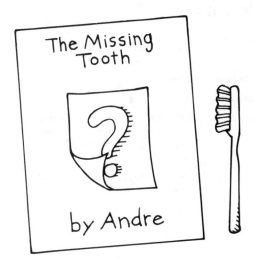

The Missing Tooth

Literature Link: *The Tooth Fairy* by Audrey Wood (CHILD'S PLAY)

Focus Word: my

Other Sight Words: have, I, is, not, the, where

Cover Art: Have students glue a white paper tooth (page 144) to their cover. Then, have students place over the tooth a paper square with a question mark on it and glue the square along one side to create a flap.

Reading Stick: Use a real toothbrush as a reading stick.

Go Up

Literature Link: *Where Do Balloons Go?: An Uplifting Mystery* by Jamie Lee Curtis (HARPERCOLLINS)

Focus Word: go

Other Sight Words: the, to, up

Cover Art: Have students color a paper balloon (page 144) and glue it to their cover. Then, give students a piece of string to glue below their balloon.

Reading Stick: Glue a real or paper balloon (page 144) to a craft stick.

Rhyming Book

Literature Link: *Ten Cats Have Hats*
by Jean Marzollo
(SCHOLASTIC)

Focus Word: with

Other Sight Words: a, is, there

Cover Art: Have students color a paper cat wearing a hat (page 144) and glue it to their cover.

Reading Stick: Glue a plastic bug, a bug sticker, or a paper bug (page 141) to a craft stick.

Who Is This From?

Literature Link: *The Secret Birthday Message*
by Eric Carle
(HARPERCOLLINS)

Focus Word: from

Other Sight Words: all, for, is, me this, who, you

Cover Art: Have students glue to their cover a rectangle cut from wrapping paper and pieces of ribbon to make a "gift."

Reading Stick: Glue curling ribbon or a paper present (page 144) to a craft stick.

School Is Out

Literature Link: *Frog and Toad Are Friends*
by Arnold Lobel
(HARPERCOLLINS)

Focus Words: is, my, there, to, with

Other Sight Words: a, do, go, I, like, the, what, you

Cover Art: Have students glue a strip of sandpaper and fish crackers to a blue cover.

Reading Stick: Glue a real or paper seashell (page 144) to a craft stick.

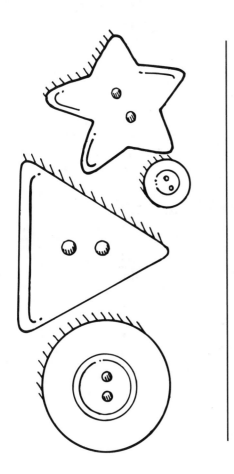
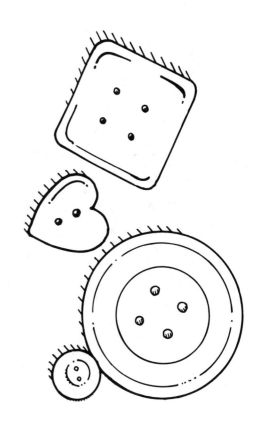

Buttons
by

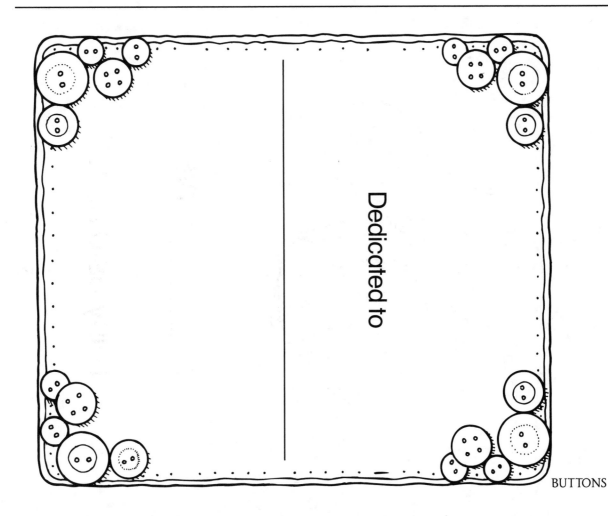

Dedicated to

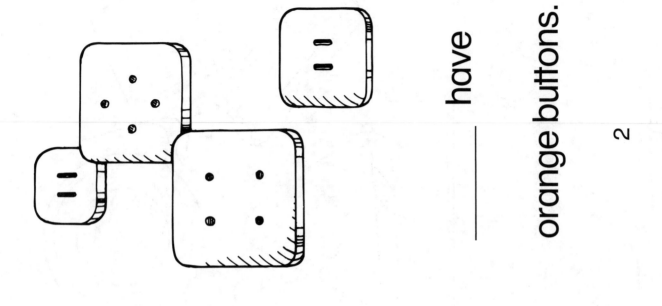

____ have

orange buttons.

2

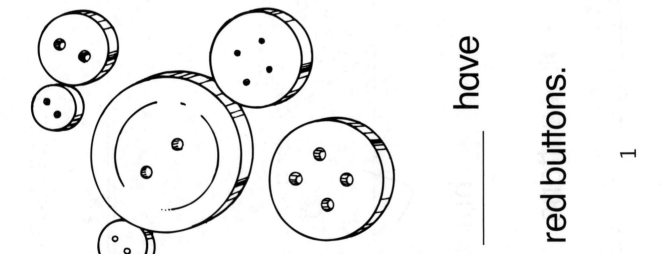

____ have

red buttons.

1

Sight Word Books: Level 1 © 2001 Creative Teaching Press

_____ have

yellow buttons.

3

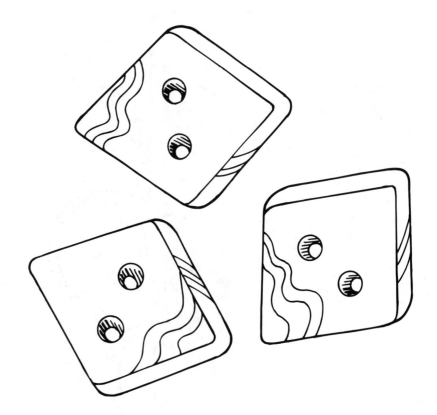

_____ have

blue buttons.

4

Sight Word Books: Level 1 © 2001 Creative Teaching Press

_____ have rainbow buttons!

The End

6

_____ have green and purple buttons.

5

Sight Word Books: Level 1 © 2001 Creative Teaching Press

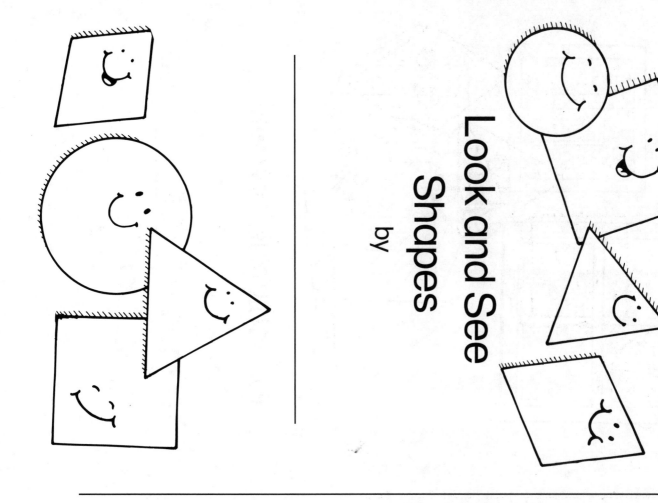

Look and See
Shapes

by

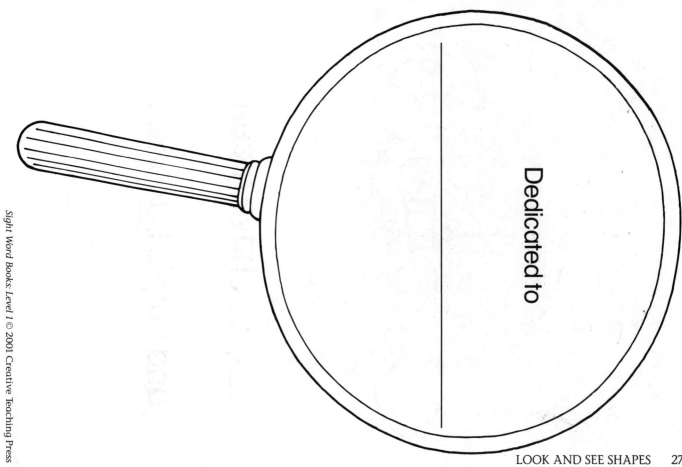

Dedicated to

We look and see what

a square _____ be.

2

We look and see what

a circle _____ be.

1

Sight Word Books: Level 1 © 2001 Creative Teaching Press

We look and see what

a triangle _____ be.

3

We look and see what

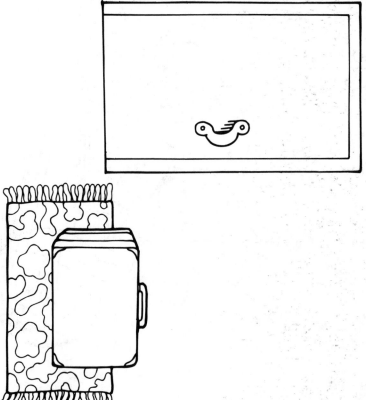

a rectangle _____ be.

4

Tell a friend what you
___ see!

The End

6

We look and see what
shapes ___ be.

5

Sight Word Books: Level 1 © 2001 Creative Teaching Press

Patterns

by

Dedicated to

There ___ patterns on the bees.

2

There ___ patterns on the flowers.

1

Sight Word Books: Level 1 © 2001 Creative Teaching Press

There _____
patterns on the birds.

3

There _____
patterns on the trees.

4

There _____ patterns on the candles when I make a wish.

The End

6

There _____ patterns on the fish.

5

Sight Word Books: Level 1 © 2001 Creative Teaching Press

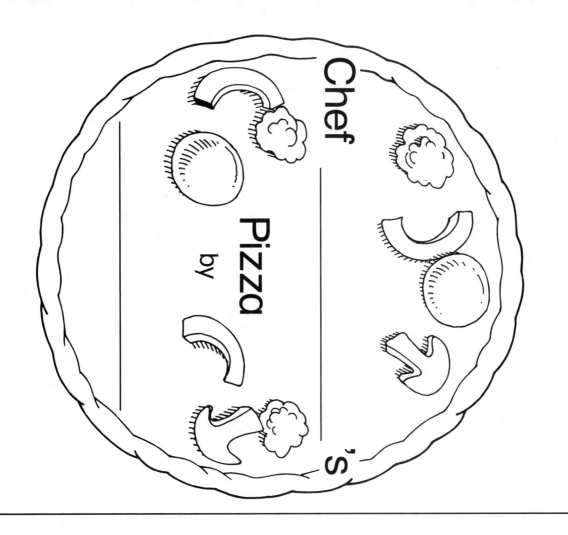

Chef _____'s

Pizza

by

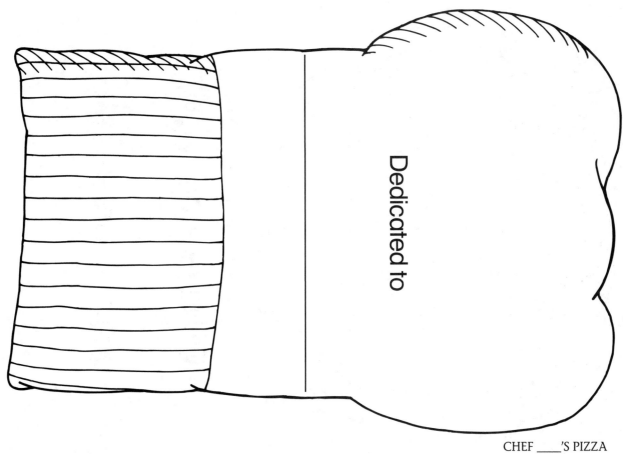

Dedicated to

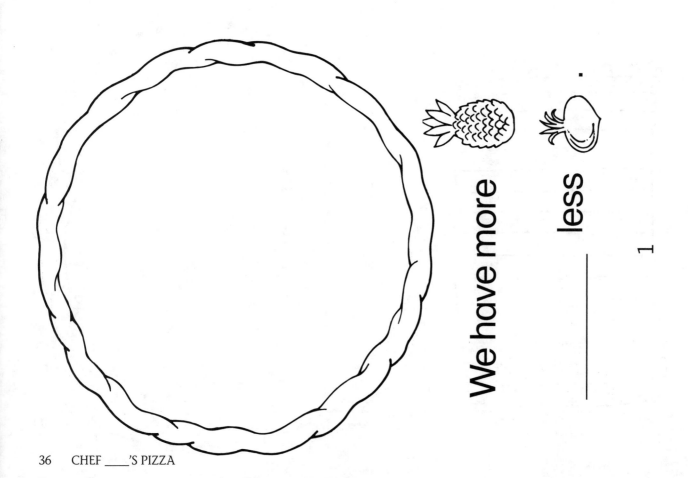

We have more _____

less _____ .

2

We have more _____

less _____ .

1

36   CHEF ____'S PIZZA

Sight Word Books: Level 1 © 2001 Creative Teaching Press

We have more _____

less 🍄🍄 .

3

We have more _____

less 🍕 .

4

CHEF _____'S PIZZA   37

Sight Word Books: Level 1 © 2001 Creative Teaching Press

CHEF ____'S PIZZA

These ____ the things ____ like on my pizza.

5

____ am hungry.

When can ____ eat?

The End

6

Sight Word Books: Level 1 © 2001 Creative Teaching Press

When I Grow Up

by

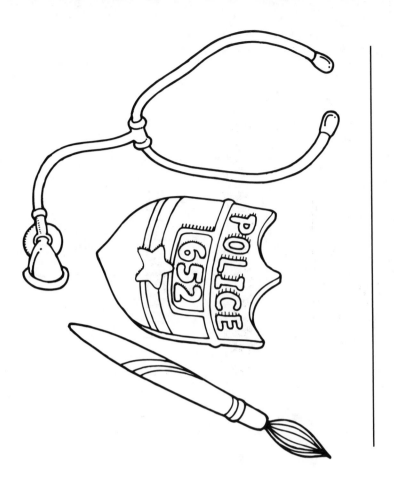

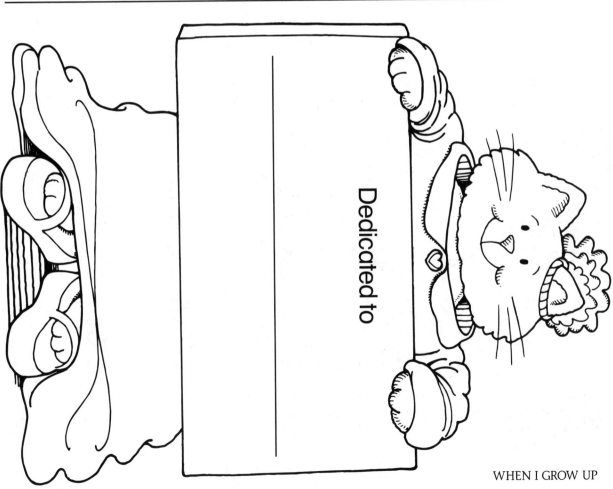

Dedicated to

I may _____
a firefighter.

2

I may _____
a doctor.

1

I may _____
an astronaut.

3

I may _____
a police officer.

4

Sight Word Books: Level 1 © 2001 Creative Teaching Press

But today I will
_____ me!

The End

6

I may _____
a teacher.

5

Sight Word Books: Level 1 © 2001 Creative Teaching Press

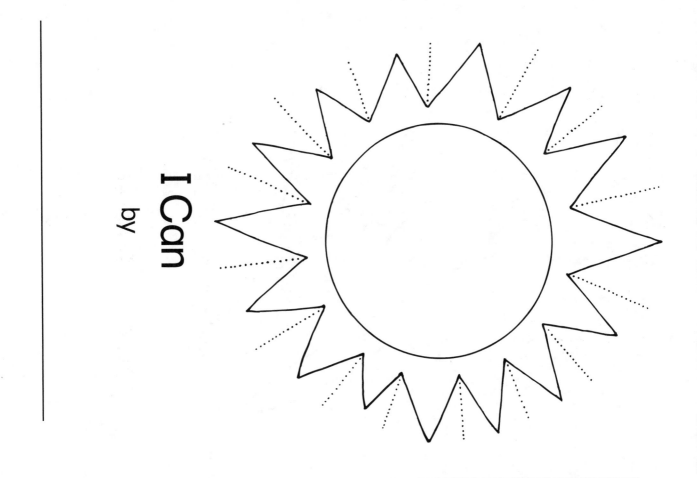

I Can

by

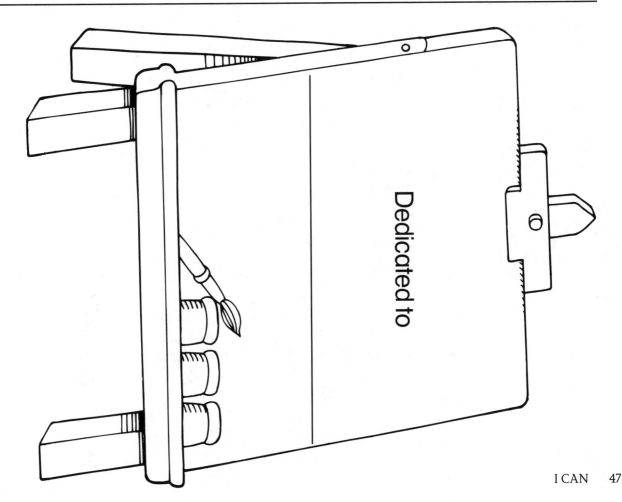

Dedicated to

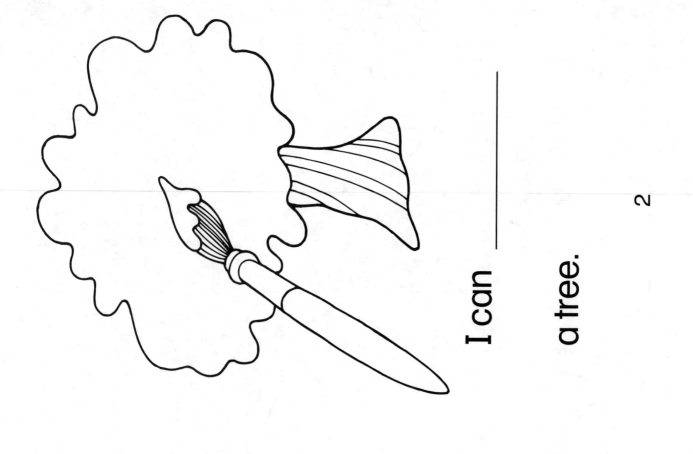

I can _____

a tree.

2

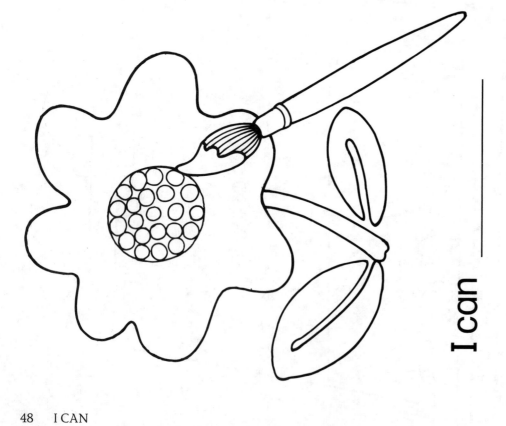

I can _____

a flower.

1

I can _____
the sun.

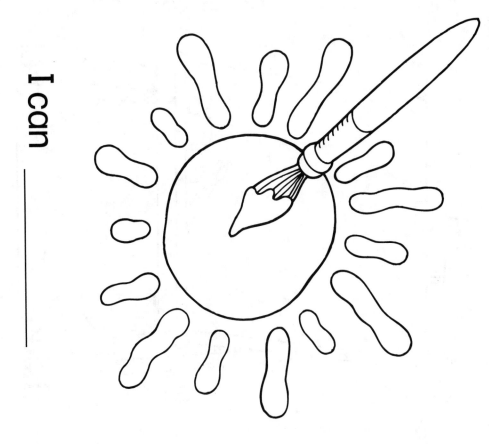

3

I can _____
a bee.

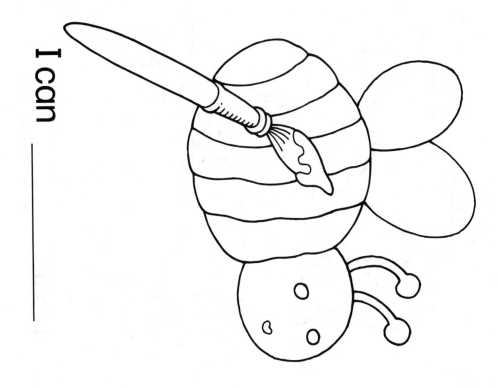

4

Sight Word Books: Level 1 © 2001 Creative Teaching Press

I can _____ me!

The End

6

I can _____

a picture.

5

Sight Word Books: Level 1 © 2001 Creative Teaching Press

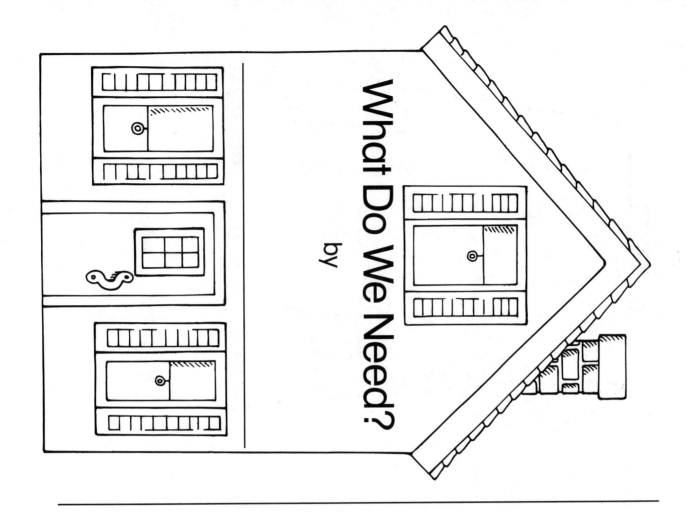

What Do We Need?

by

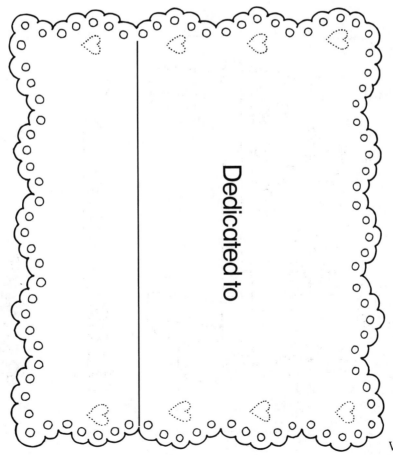

Dedicated to

Do we need clothes?

Yes, we _____ !

2

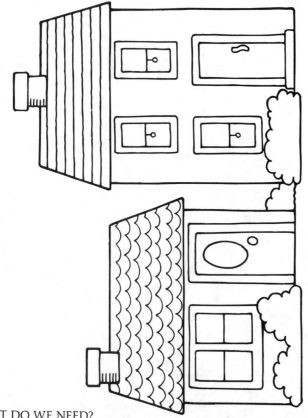

Do we need houses?

Yes, we _____ !

1

Sight Word Books: Level 1 © 2001 Creative Teaching Press

Do we need water?

Yes, we _____ !

3

Do we need food?

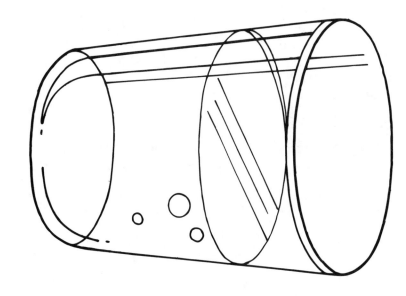

Yes, we _____ !

4

Do we need love?

Yes, we _____ !

The End

6

Do we need friends?

Yes, we _____ !

5

Sight Word Books: Level 1 © 2001 Creative Teaching Press

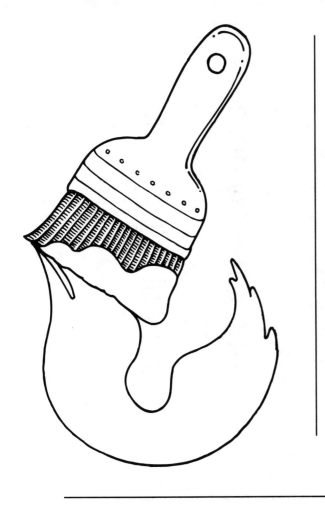

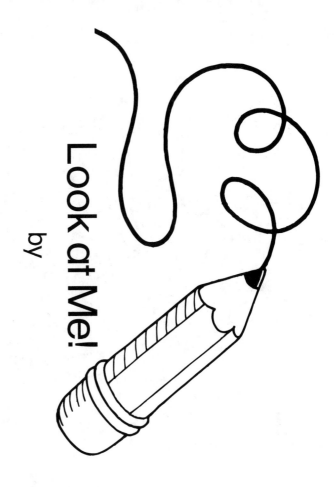

Look at Me!

by

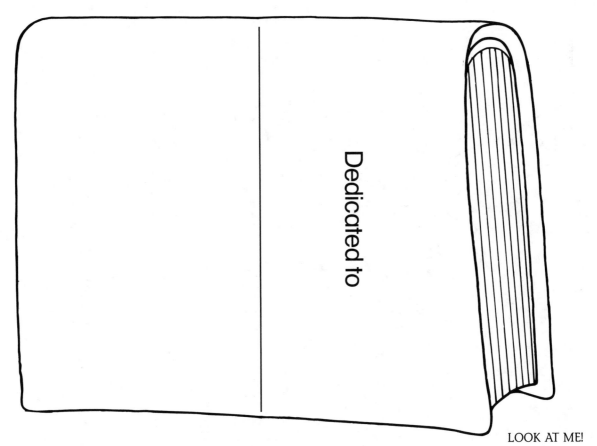

Dedicated to

Sight Word Books: Level 1 © 2001 Creative Teaching Press

I can write my name.

Look at _____ !

2

_____ at

what I can do.

1

Sight Word Books: Level 1 © 2001 Creative Teaching Press

I can _____ a

snowman. Look at _____ !

3

I can make a rainbow.

Look at _____ !

4

Sight Word Books: Level 1 © 2001 Creative Teaching Press

I can read this book.

Look at _____ !

The End

6

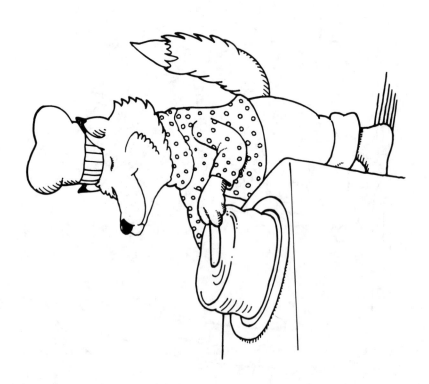

I can _____ a _____ !

cake. Look at _____

5

Sight Word Books: Level 1 © 2001 Creative Teaching Press

Watch My
Garden Grow

by

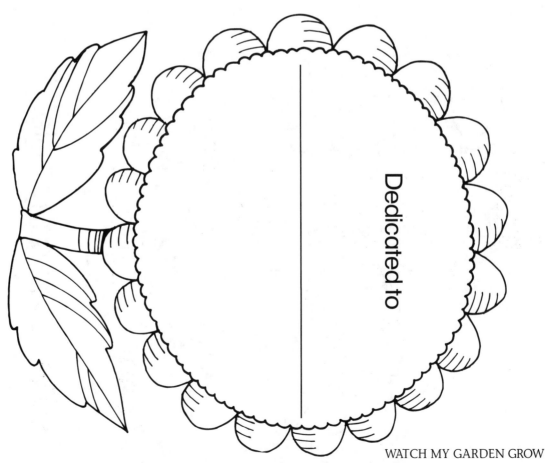

Dedicated to

_____ plant the seeds.

2

_____ dig the hole.

1

Sight Word Books: Level 1 © 2001 Creative Teaching Press

_____ see the sun.

3

_____ water the soil.

4

Sight Word Books: Level 1 © 2001 Creative Teaching Press

watch my garden grow.

The End

6

pull the weeds.

5

Sight Word Books: Level 1 © 2001 Creative Teaching Press

Rain

by _____

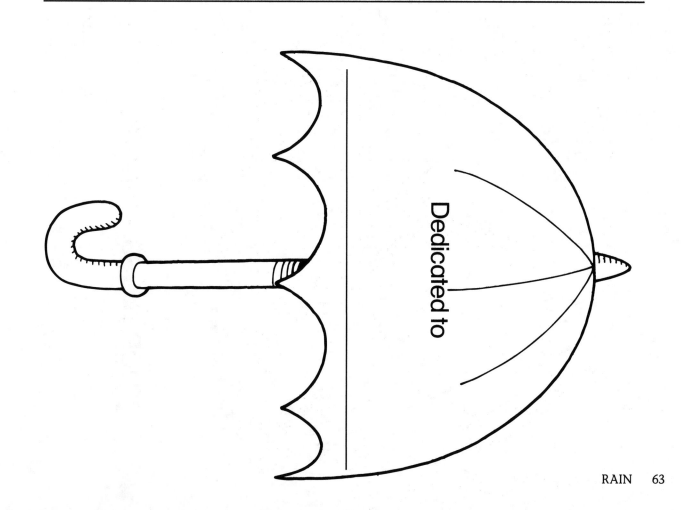

Dedicated to _____

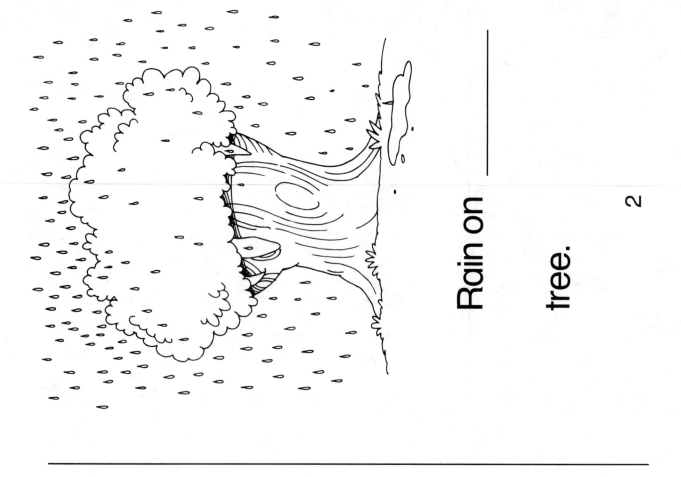

Rain on

tree.

2

Rain on

green grass.

1

Sight Word Books: Level 1 © 2001 Creative Teaching Press

Rain on _____ flower.

3

Rain on _____ bee.

4

But not on me!

The End

6

Rain on _____
rooftop.

5

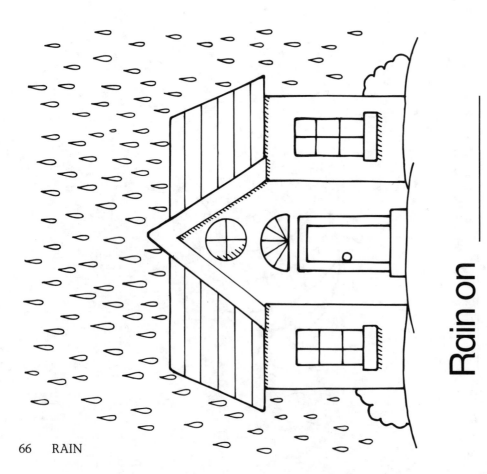

Sight Word Books: Level 1 © 2001 Creative Teaching Press

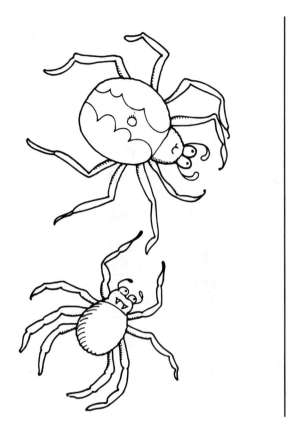

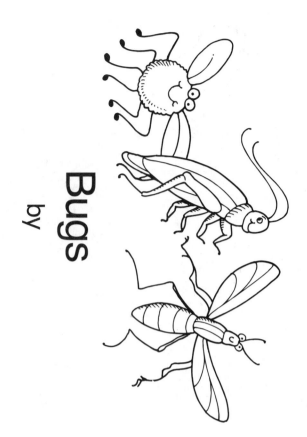

Bugs
by

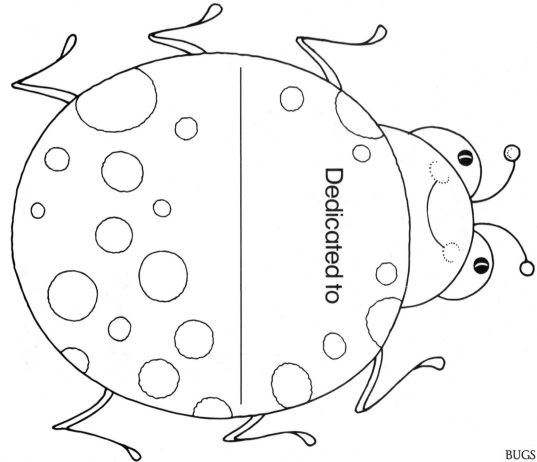

Dedicated to

Where _____
that little bug?

2

Where _____
that big bug?

1

Sight Word Books: Level 1 © 2001 Creative Teaching Press

Where _____
that mean bug?

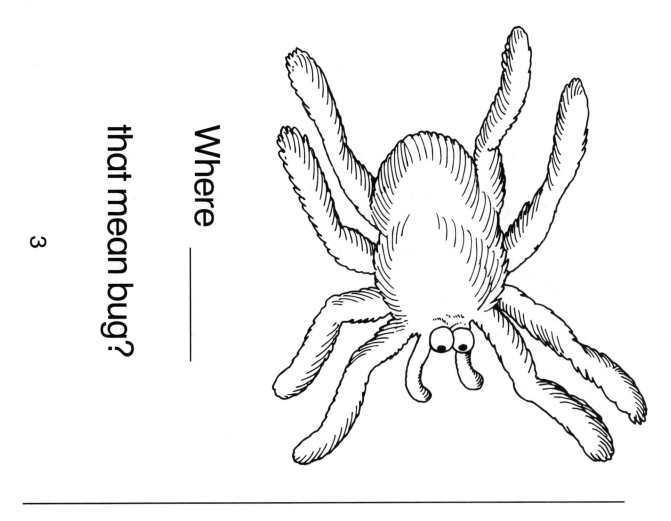

3

Where _____
that nice bug?

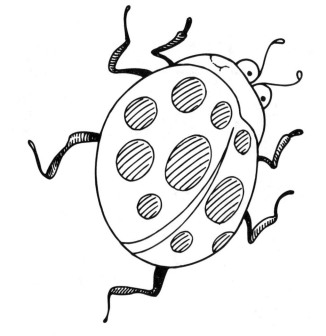

4

Sight Word Books: Level 1 © 2001 Creative Teaching Press

There it ____ .

Swat!

The End

6

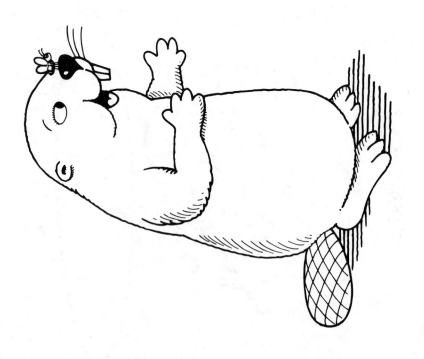

Where ____

that pesky bug?

5

Sight Word Books: Level 1 © 2001 Creative Teaching Press

Matter
by

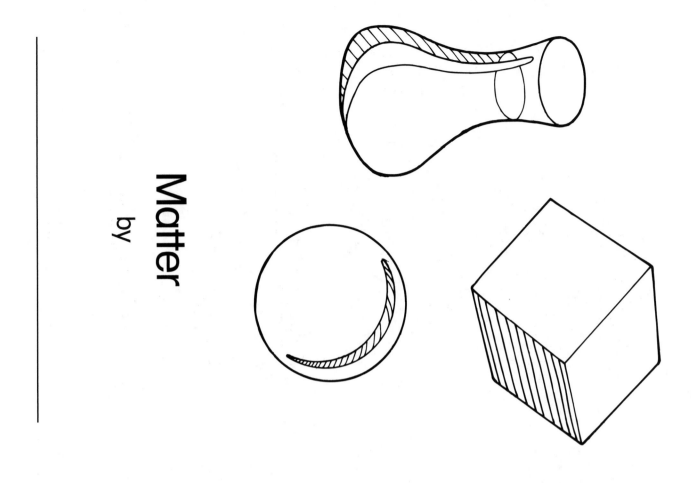

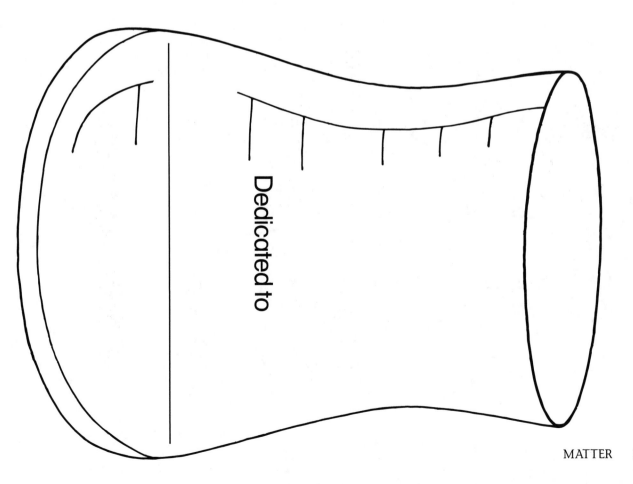

Dedicated to

Sight Word Books: Level 1 © 2001 Creative Teaching Press

This is ___ bee.

2

This is ___ flower.

1

Sight Word Books: Level 1 © 2001 Creative Teaching Press

This is ___ house.

3

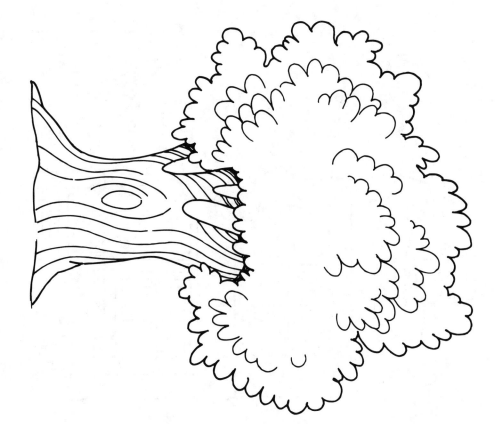

This is ___ tree.

4

even me!

The End

6

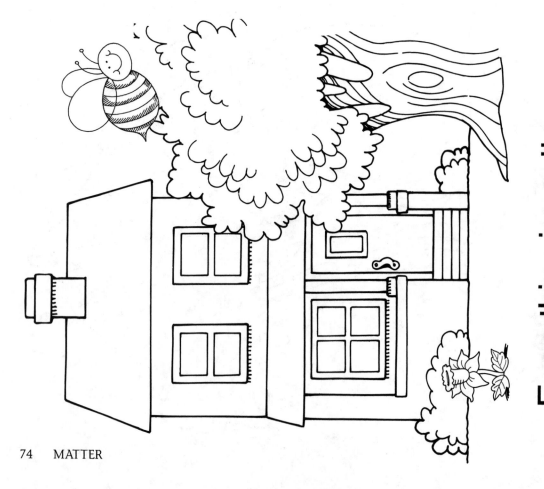

Everything is matter—

5

Sight Word Books: Level 1 © 2001 Creative Teaching Press

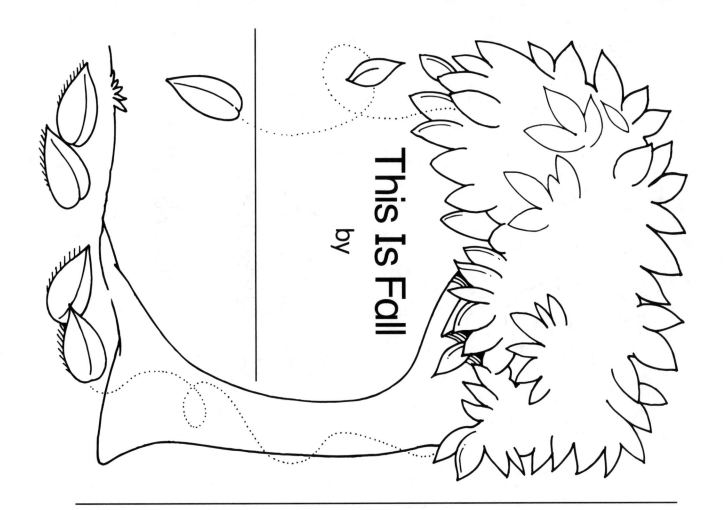

This Is Fall

by

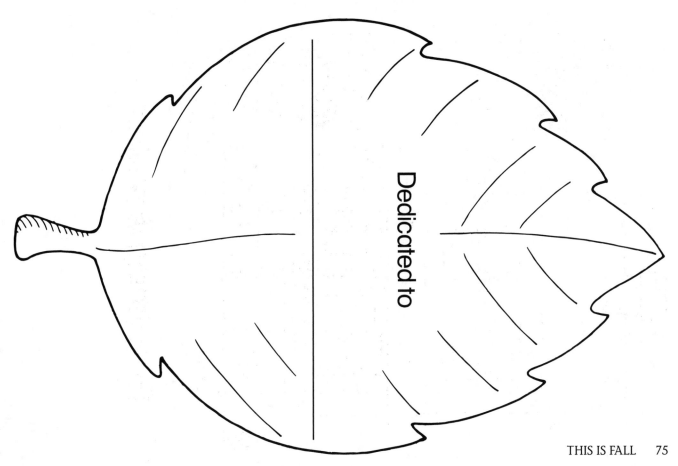

Dedicated to

_____ that big tree.

2

see the leaves

1

Sight Word Books: Level 1 © 2001 Creative Teaching Press

_____ will sit
the ground.

3

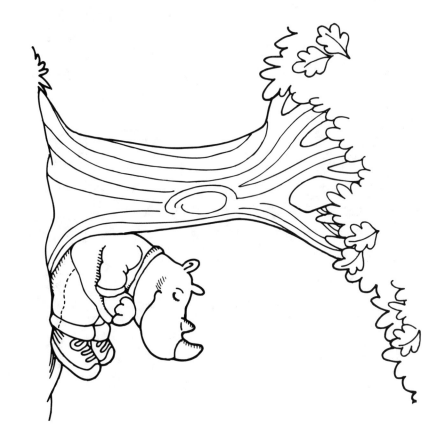

The leaves
_____ the tree

4

Sight Word Books: Level 1 © 2001 Creative Teaching Press

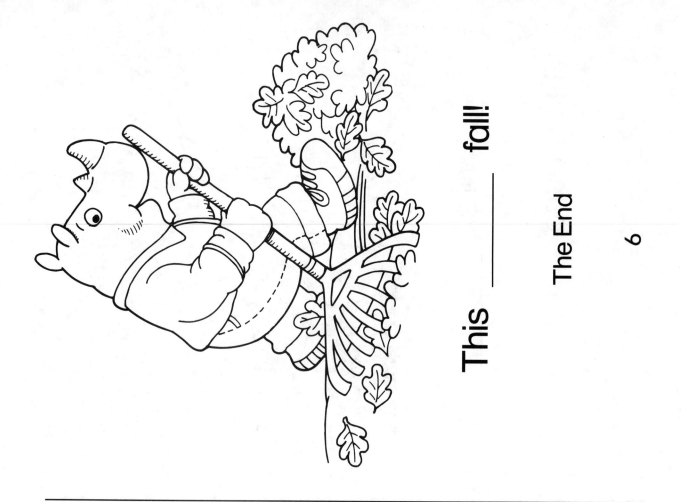

This _____ fall!

The End

6

fall down _____ me.

5

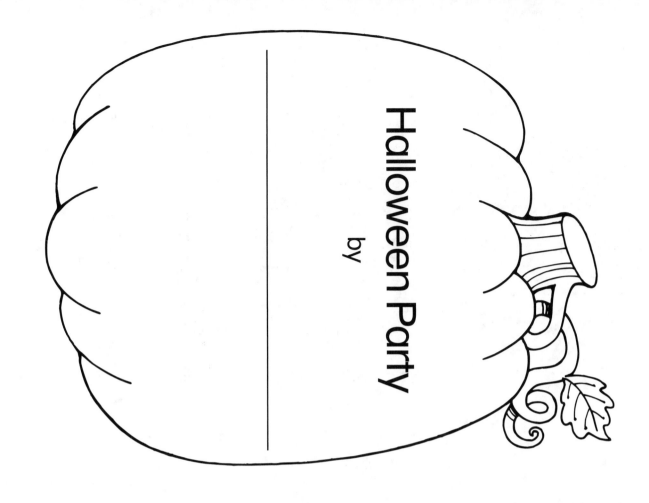

Halloween Party

by

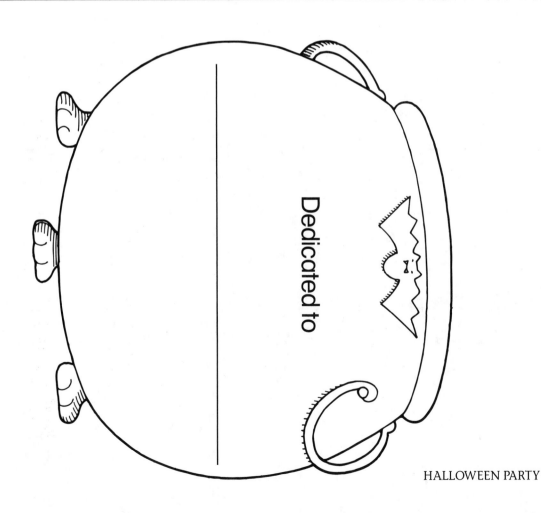

Dedicated to

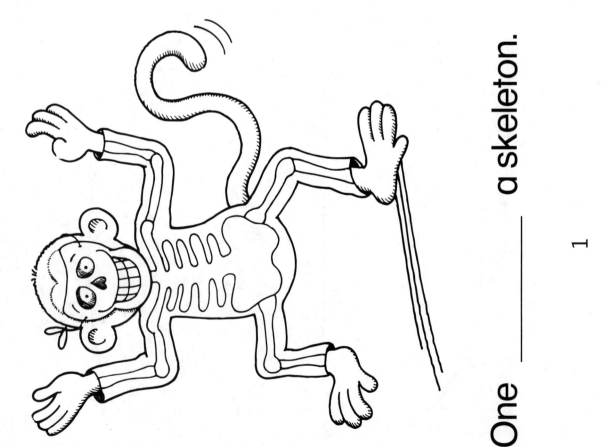

One _____ a bat.

2

One _____ a skeleton.

1

Sight Word Books: Level 1 © 2001 Creative Teaching Press

One _____ a monster.

3

One _____ a cat.

4

Which one do you like most?

The End

6

One _____ a ghost.

5

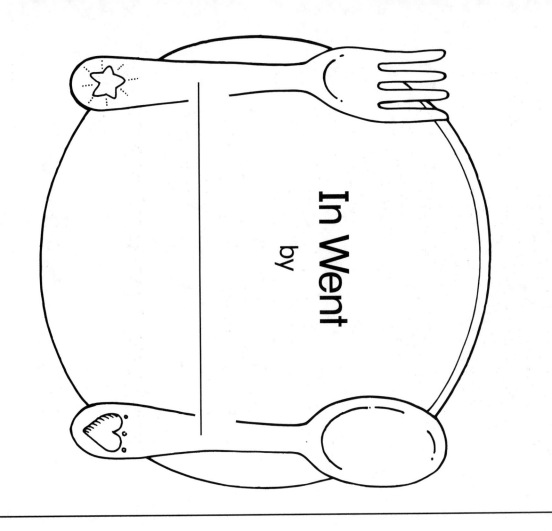

In Went
by

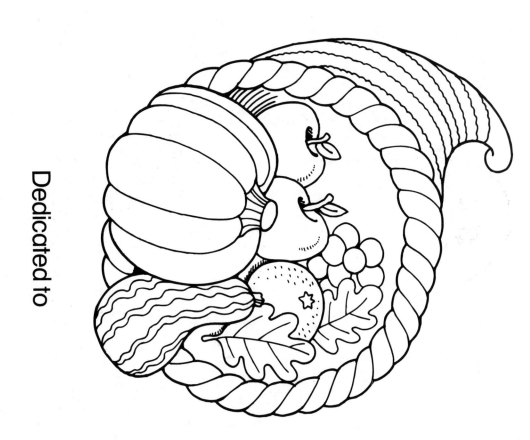

Dedicated to

went the corn.

2

went the potatoes.

1

Sight Word Books: Level 1 © 2001 Creative Teaching Press

went the turkey.

3

went the stuffing.

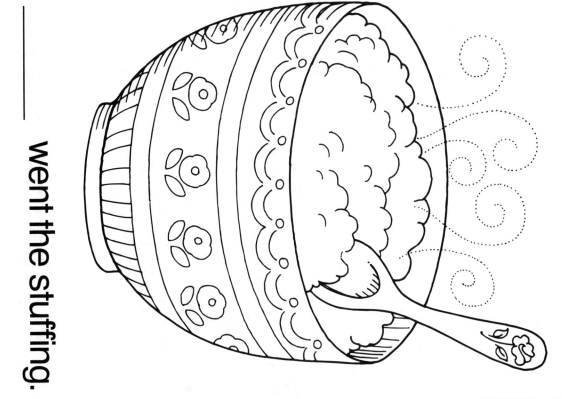

4

Now I am full!

The End

6

---

went the rolls.

5

Sight Word Books: Level 1 © 2001 Creative Teaching Press

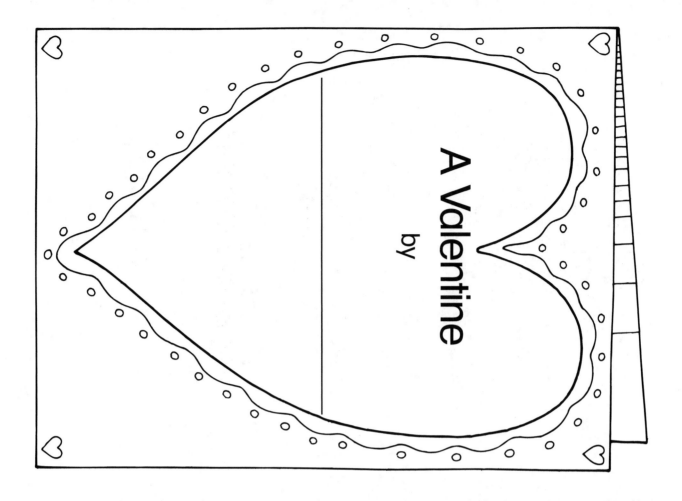

A Valentine

by

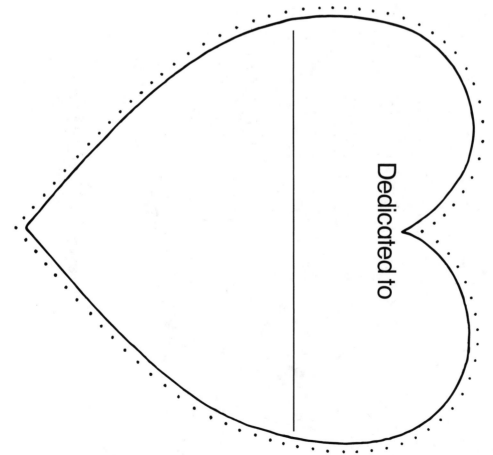

Dedicated to

could be pink.

2

could be red.

1

Sight Word Books: Level 1 © 2001 Creative Teaching Press

———— could be green.

3

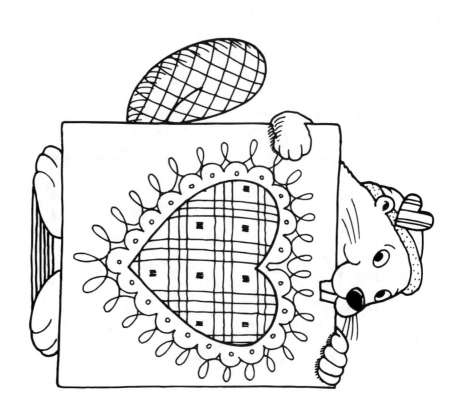

———— could be blue.

4

just for you!

The End

6

This one is a valentine

5

Sight Word Books: Level 1 © 2001 Creative Teaching Press

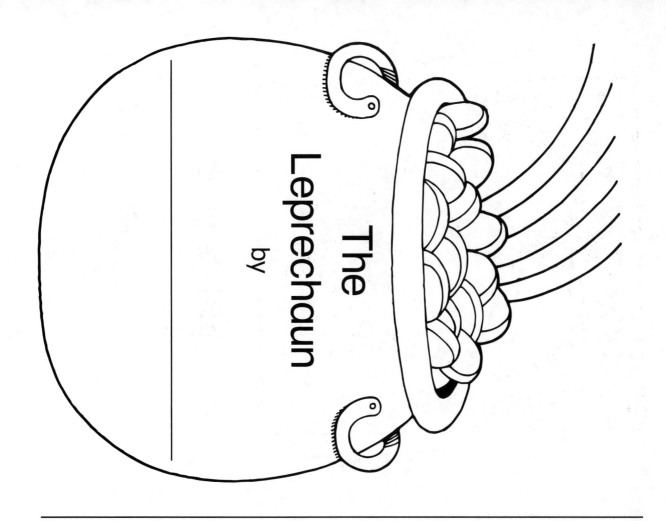

The Leprechaun

by _____

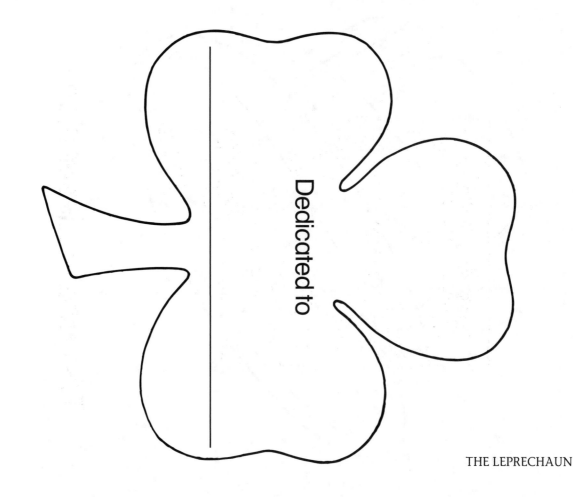

Dedicated to _____

_____ is orange.

2

_____ is black.

1

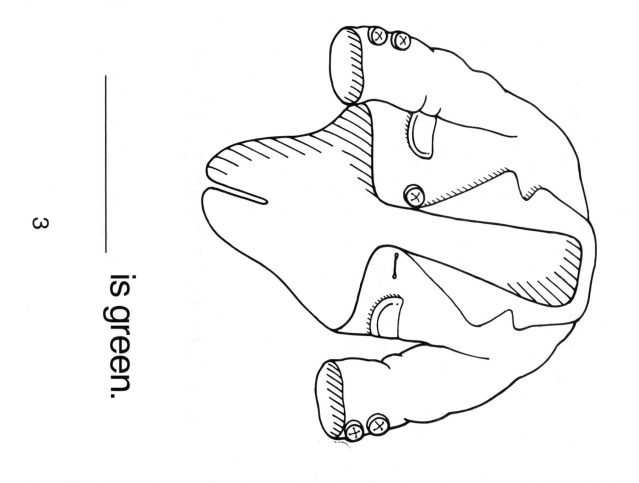

_____ is green.

3

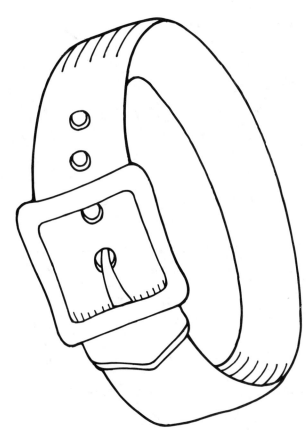

_____ is brown.

4

Sight Word Books: Level 1 © 2001 Creative Teaching Press

is a

leprechaun for me to hold!

The End

6

is gold.

5

Sight Word Books: Level 1 © 2001 Creative Teaching Press

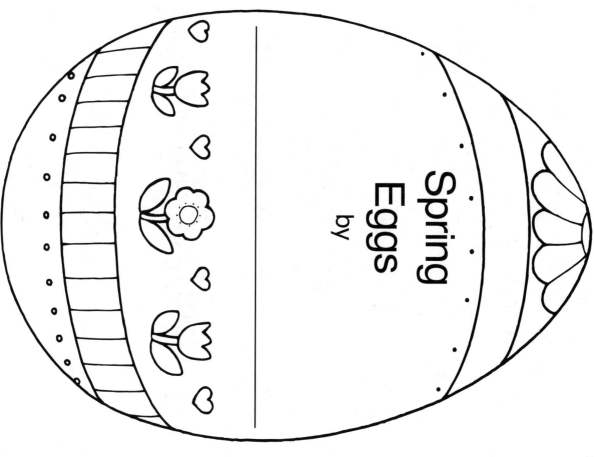

Spring
Eggs
by

Dedicated to

Here is one for hen.

_____ is red.

2

Here _____ one for

duck. It is yellow.

1

Here ____ ____ one for turtle.

____ ____ is green.

3

It ____ ____ is one for snake.

____ ____ orange.

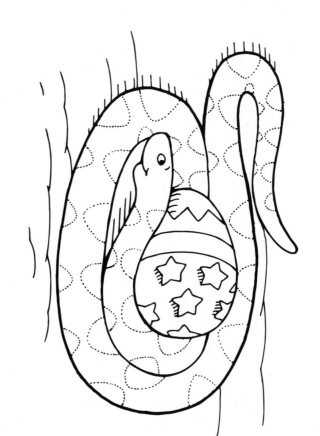

4

It _____ blue!

The End

6

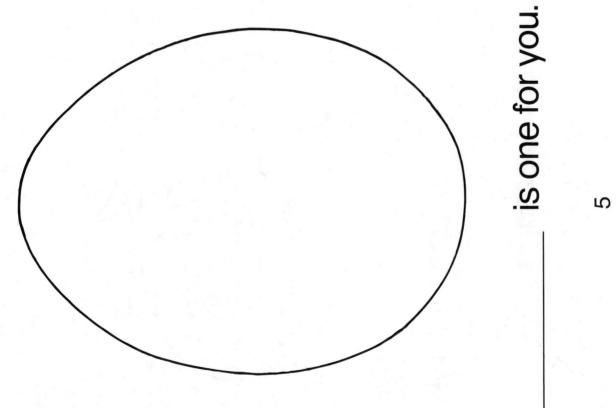

_____ is one for you.

5

A Jungle
Good Morning

by

Dedicated to

I say "good morning"

the giraffe.

2

I say "good morning"

the lion.

1

Sight Word Books: Level 1 © 2001 Creative Teaching Press

I say "good morning"

_____ the elephant.

3

I say "good morning"

_____ the snake.

4

Sight Word Books: Level 1 © 2001 Creative Teaching Press

I say "good morning" _____
the jungle in room _____ .

The End

6

I say "good morning" _____
the crocodile.

5

Sight Word Books: Level 1 © 2001 Creative Teaching Press

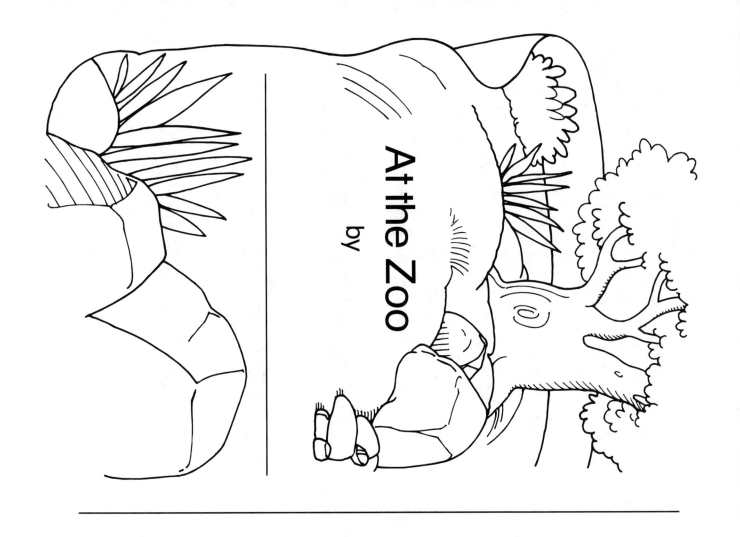

At the Zoo

by

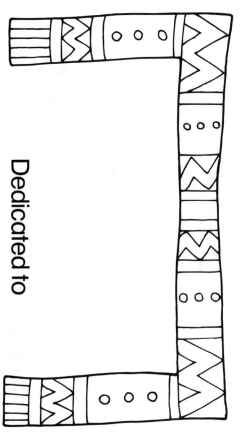

Dedicated to

Lion, lion, where

are you? _____

I see you at the zoo?

2

Snake, snake, where

are you? _____

I see you at the zoo?

1

Sight Word Books: Level 1 © 2001 Creative Teaching Press

Zebra, zebra, where

are you? _____

I see you at the zoo?

3

Monkey, monkey, where

are you? _____

I see you at the zoo?

4

Sight Word Books: Level 1 © 2001 Creative Teaching Press

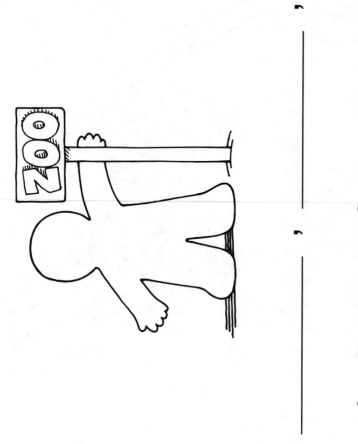

where are you?

I see you at the zoo?

The End

6

Elephant, elephant, where

are you?

I see you at the zoo?

5

Sight Word Books: Level 1 © 2001 Creative Teaching Press

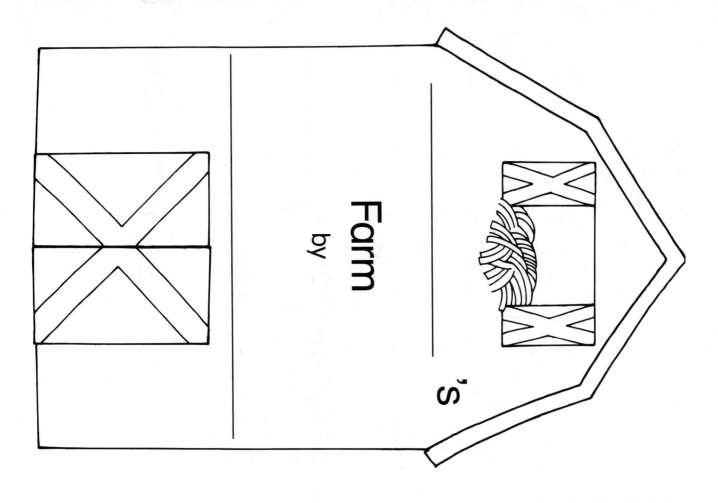

Farm

by

_____

's

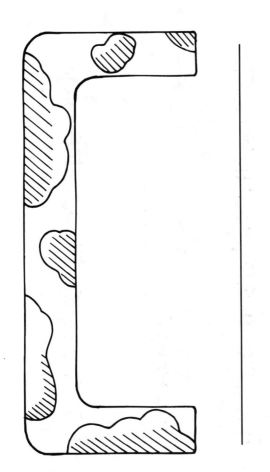

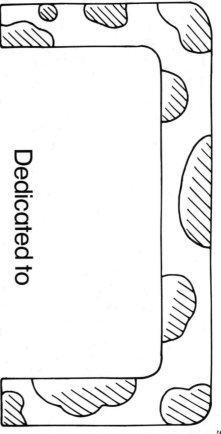

Dedicated to

_____

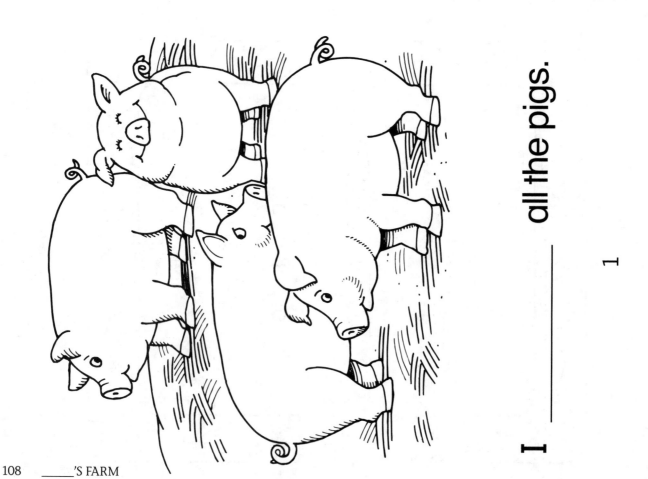

all the cows.

I

2

all the pigs.

I

1

Sight Word Books: Level 1 © 2001 Creative Teaching Press

I ____ all the ducks.

3

I ____ all the horses.

4

I _____ all the

chicks that peep, peep, peep!

The End

6

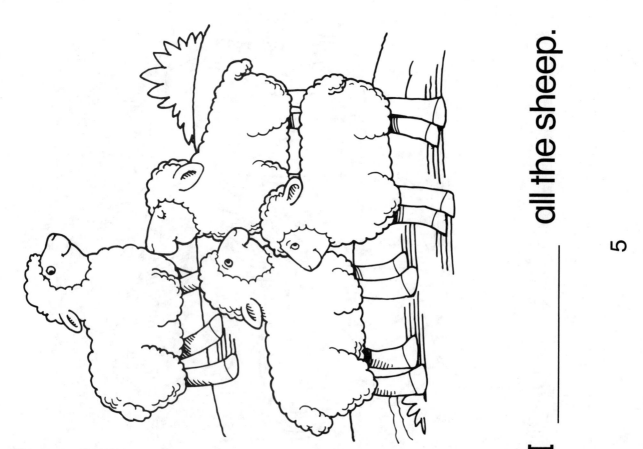

I _____ all the sheep.

5

Sight Word Books: Level 1 © 2001 Creative Teaching Press

An Alligator

by

Dedicated to

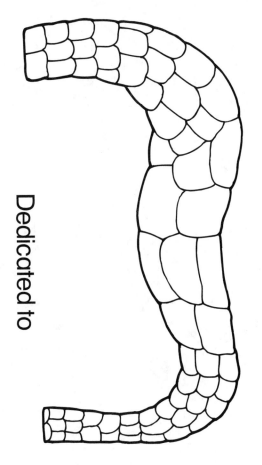

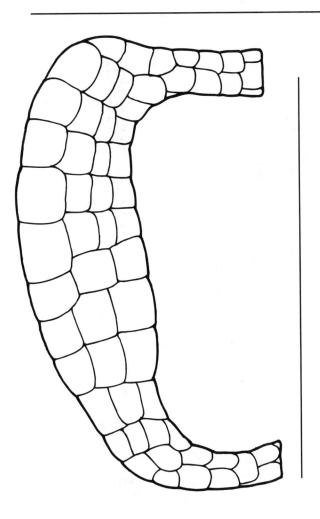

An alligator _____ teeth.

1

An alligator _____ a tail.

2

Sight Word Books: Level 1 © 2001 Creative Teaching Press

An alligator _____ claws.

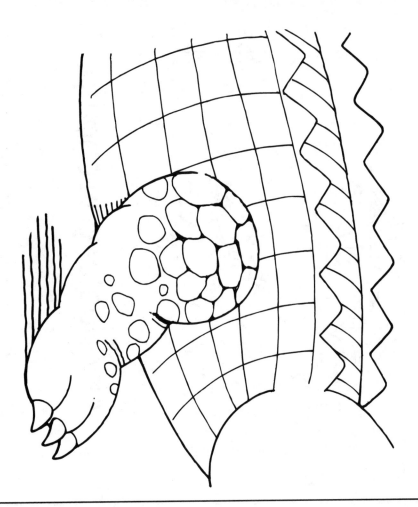

3

An alligator _____ scales.

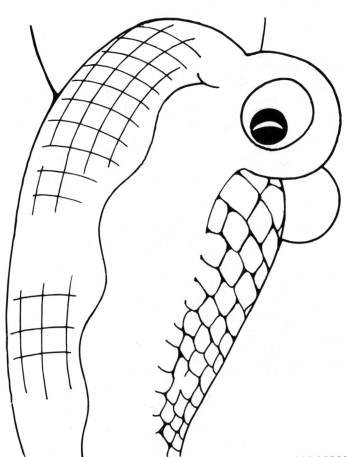

4

Sight Word Books: Level 1 © 2001 Creative Teaching Press

An alligator can chomp,

chomp, chomp!

The End

6

An alligator _____

a home in the swamp.

5

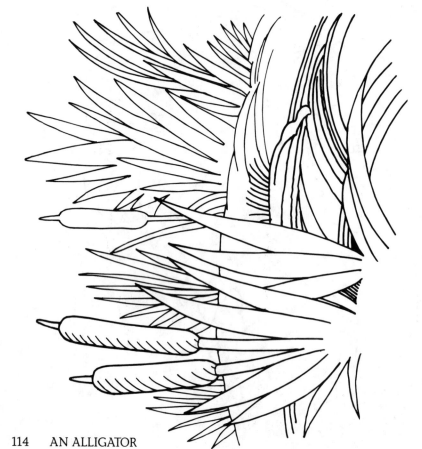

Sight Word Books: Level 1 © 2001 Creative Teaching Press

All Penguins

by

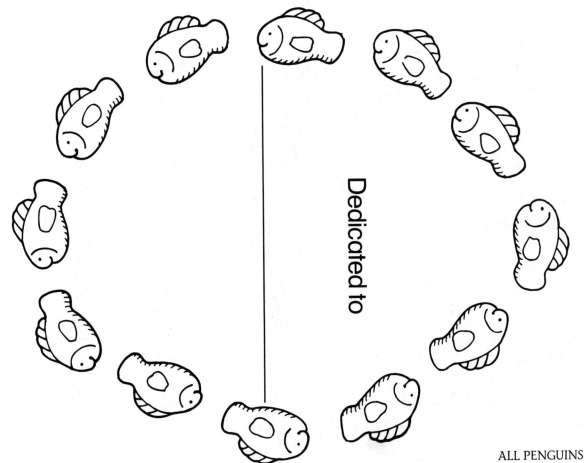

Dedicated to

_____ penguins
like to play.

2

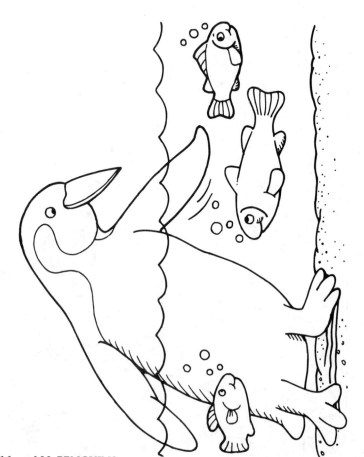

_____ penguins
like to fish.

1

_____ penguins

_____ to run.

3

_____ penguins

like _____ dive.

4

Sight Word Books: Level 1 © 2001 Creative Teaching Press

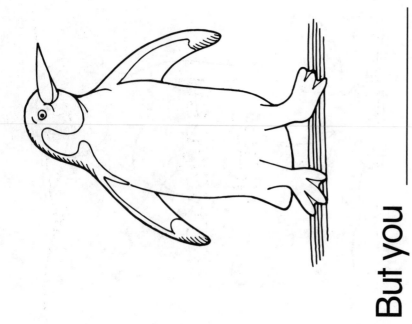

But you _____

never see a penguin fly!

The End

6

_____ penguins

_____ to slide.

5

Sight Word Books: Level 1 © 2001 Creative Teaching Press

The Missing Tooth

by

Dedicated to

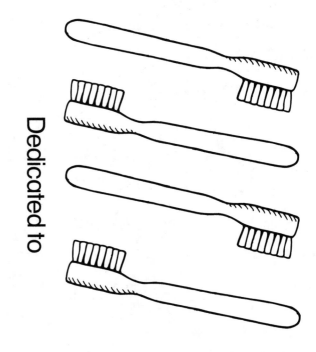

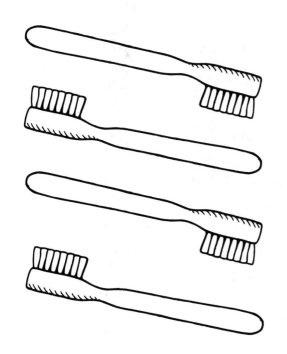

Where is _____ tooth?

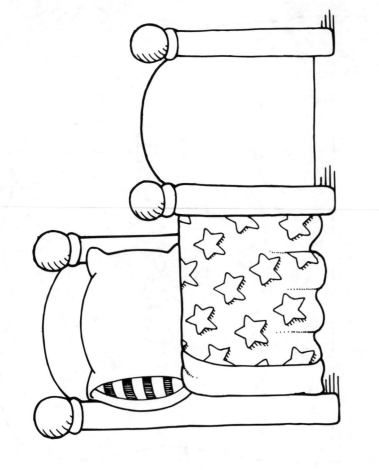

1

_____ tooth is

not under the bed.

2

Sight Word Books: Level 1 © 2001 Creative Teaching Press

_____ tooth is

not under the chair.

3

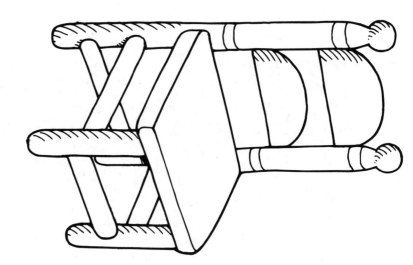

_____ tooth is

not under the bear.

4

Sight Word Books: Level 1 © 2001 Creative Teaching Press

I have your tooth!

The End

6

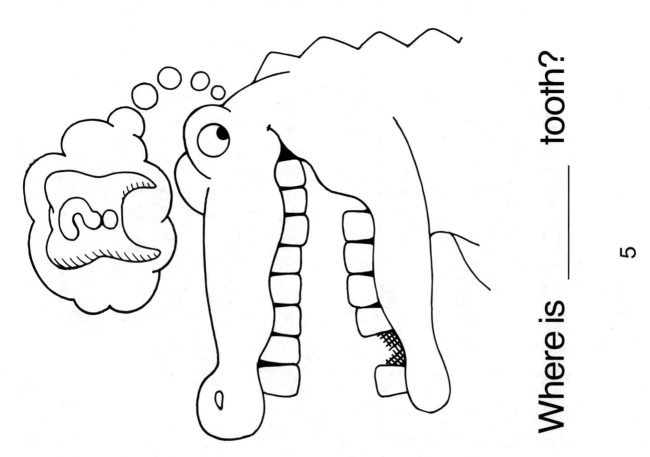

Where is _____ tooth?

5

Sight Word Books: Level 1 © 2001 Creative Teaching Press

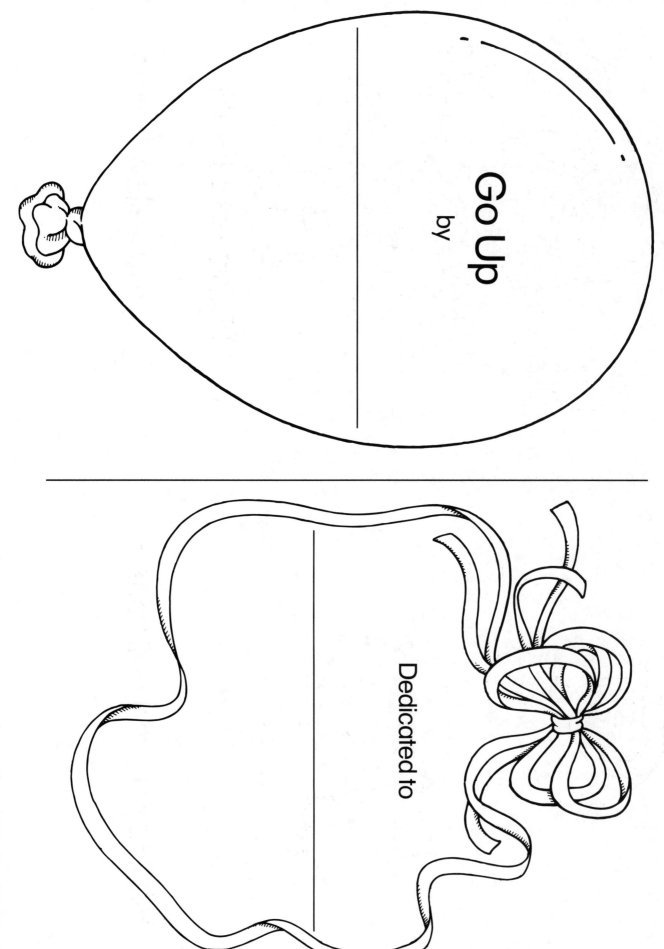

Go Up

by

Dedicated to

_____ up yellow balloon.

2

_____ up red balloon.

1

Sight Word Books: Level 1 © 2001 Creative Teaching Press

_____ up green balloon.

3

_____ up blue balloon.

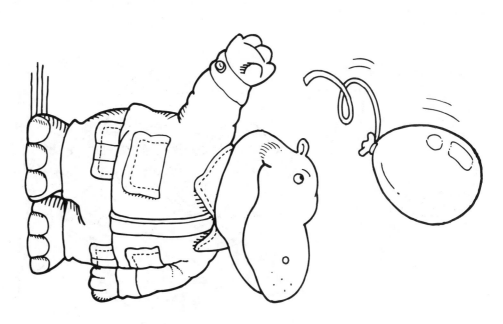

4

up to the moon.

The End

6

---

up orange balloon.

5

Sight Word Books: Level 1 © 2001 Creative Teaching Press

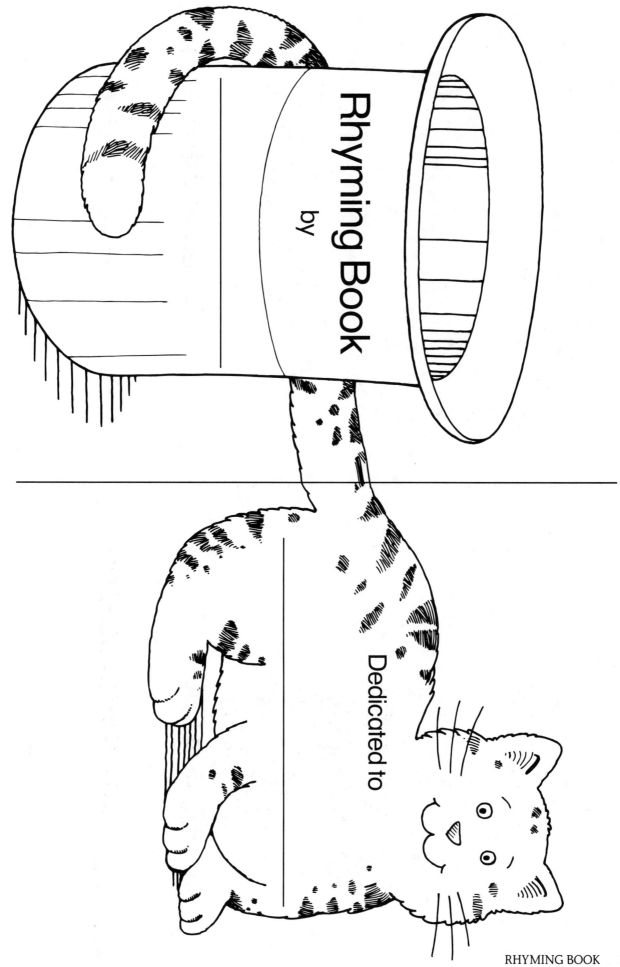

Rhyming Book

by

Dedicated to

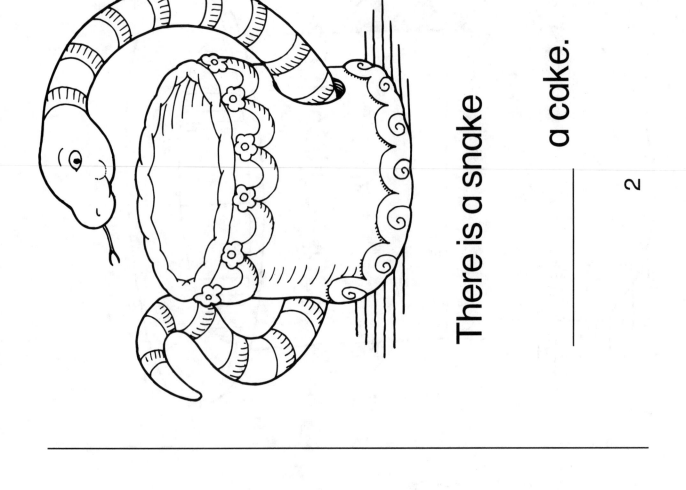

There is a snake _____

a cake.

2

_____

There is a cat _____

a hat.

1

Sight Word Books: Level 1 © 2001 Creative Teaching Press

There is a frog

_____ a log.

3

There is a fly

_____ a tie.

4

Sight Word Books: Level 1 © 2001 Creative Teaching Press

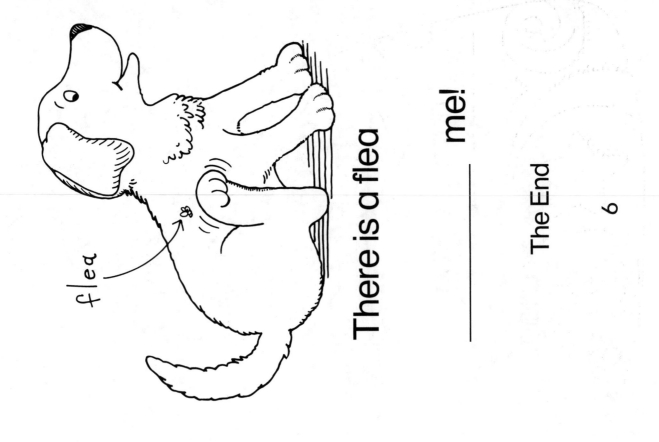

flea

There is a flea

me!

The End

6

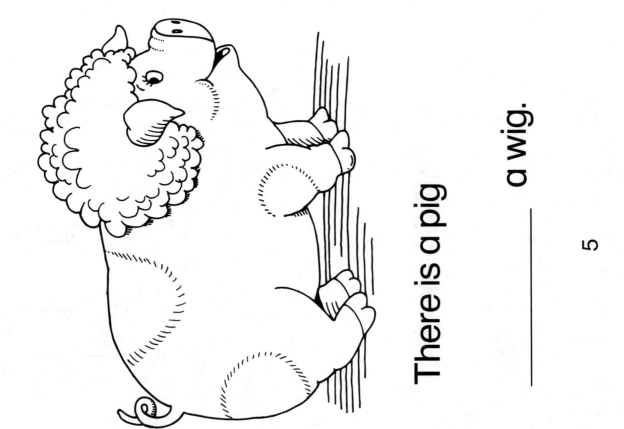

There is a pig

a wig.

5

Sight Word Books: Level 1 © 2001 Creative Teaching Press

Who Is
This From?
by

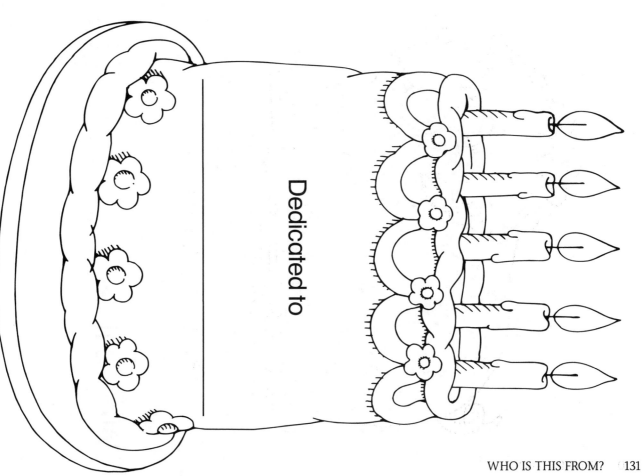

Dedicated to

Who is this _____ ?

2

Who is this _____ ?

1

Who is this _____ ?

3

Who is this _____ ?

4

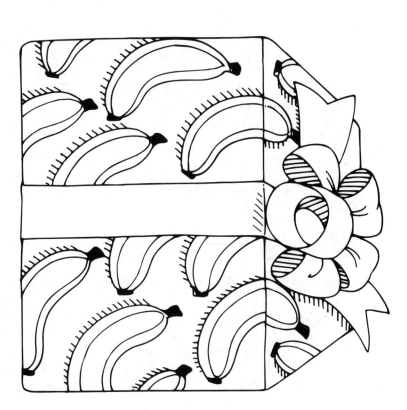

All for me? Thank you!

The End

6

Who is this _____?

5

School
Is Out

by

Dedicated to

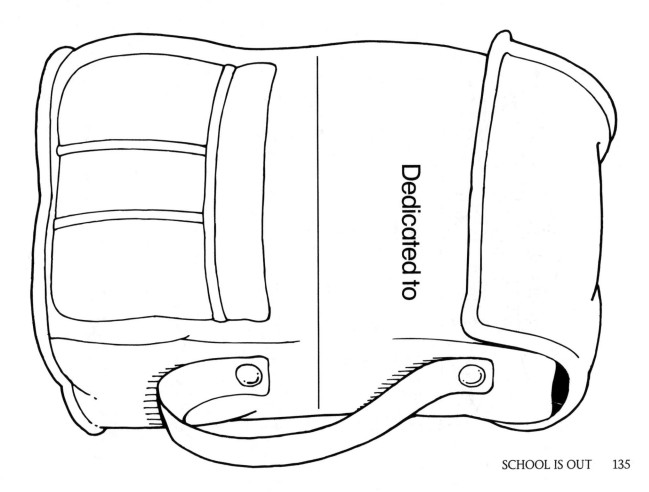

I go _____ my friends

to the park.

is a lot to do.

2

I go with my friends to

the beach. _____

is a lot to do.

1

I _____ with my friends to

the museum.

_____ is a lot to do.

3

I go with _____ friends

to the fair. _____

_____ is a lot to do.

4

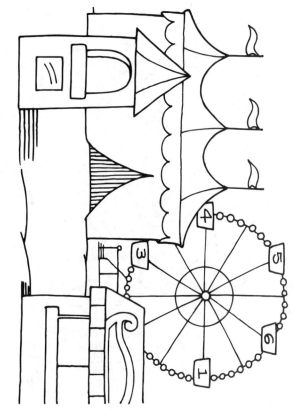

Having Fun with My Friends

School _____ out. What _____ do?

would you like

The End

6

I go _____

my friends to the zoo.

_____ is a lot to do.

5

Math Patterns

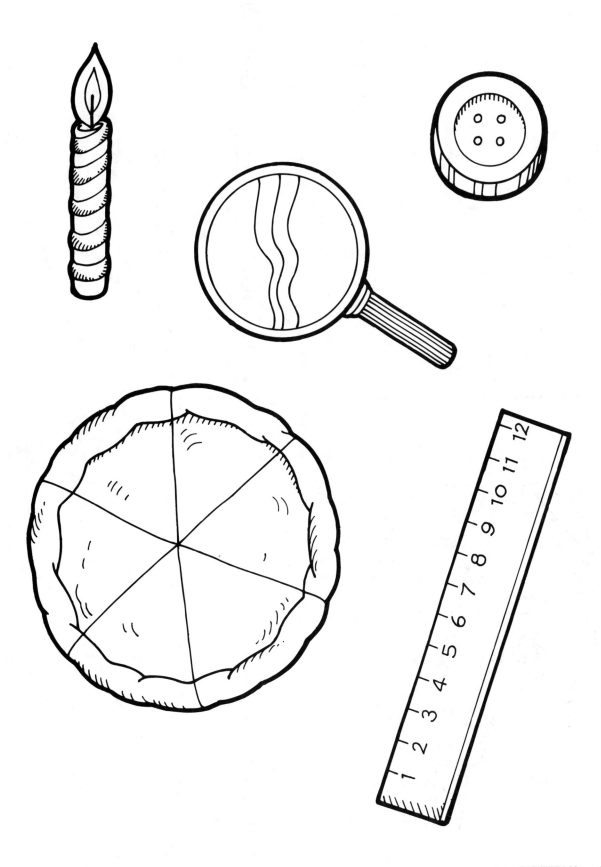

Self-Esteem Patterns

Science Patterns

Seasonal/Holiday Patterns

Animal Patterns

Just for Fun Patterns

Sight Word Books: Level 1 © 2001 Creative Teaching Press